Dear Parent:

Congratulations! Your child is taking the first steps on an exciting journey. The destination? Independent reading!

STEP INTO READING® will help your child get there. The program offers books at five levels that accompany children from their first attempts at reading to reading success. Each step includes fun stories, fiction and nonfiction, and colorful art. There are also Step into Reading Sticker Books, Step into Reading Math Readers, Step into Reading Write-In Readers, Step into Reading Phonics Readers, and Step into Reading Phonics First Steps! Boxed Sets—a complete literacy program with something to interest every child.

Learning to Read, Step by Step!

Ready to Read   Preschool–Kindergarten
• big type and easy words • rhyme and rhythm • picture clues
For children who know the alphabet and are eager to begin reading.

Reading with Help   Preschool–Grade 1
• basic vocabulary • short sentences • simple stories
For children who recognize familiar words and sound out new words with help.

Reading on Your Own   Grades 1–3
• engaging characters • easy-to-follow plots • popular topics
For children who are ready to read on their own.

Reading Paragraphs   Grades 2–3
• challenging vocabulary • short paragraphs • exciting stories
For newly independent readers who read simple sentences with confidence.

Ready for Chapters   Grades 2–4
• chapters • longer paragraphs • full-color art
For children who want to take the plunge into chapter books but still like colorful pictures.

STEP INTO READING® is designed to give every child a successful reading experience. The grade levels are only guides. Children can progress through the steps at their own speed, developing confidence in their reading, no matter what their grade.

Remember, a lifetime love of reading starts with a single step!

For René, Nancy, Jessica, Vicki, Michele, and Shari,
my dearest and most loyal girlfriends, who are each
as unique and amazing as the playful platypus
—G.L.C.

For my daughters, Anna and Claire,
as always, and Bob the cat,
who posed for the art showing platypus size
—P.M.

Text copyright © 2004 by Ginjer L. Clarke. Illustrations copyright © 2004 by Paul Mirocha.
All rights reserved under International and Pan-American Copyright Conventions. Published
in the United States by Random House Children's Books, a division of Random House, Inc.,
New York, and simultaneously in Canada by Random House of Canada Limited, Toronto.

www.stepintoreading.com

Educators and librarians, for a variety of teaching tools, visit us at
www.randomhouse.com/teachers

Library of Congress Cataloging-in-Publication Data
Clarke, Ginjer L.
Platypus! / by Ginjer L. Clarke ; illustrated by Paul Mirocha. —
   p.   cm. — (Step into reading. A step 2 book)
SUMMARY: Simply describes what a platypus looks like, where it lives, and how it swims,
builds a nest, cares for its eggs, and raises its babies.
ISBN 0-375-82417-0 (trade) — ISBN 0-375-92417-5 (lib. bdg.)
1. Platypus—Juvenile literature. [1. Platypus.]
I. Mirocha, Paul, ill. II. Title. III. Series.
QL737 .M72 C53 2004 599.2'9—dc22 2003016512

Printed in the United States of America 10 9 8 7 6 5 4 3 2 1 First Edition

Platypus!

by Ginjer L. Clarke

illustrated by Paul Mirocha

Random House New York

The sun is setting.
Many animals are
going to sleep.

But the platypus
(say: PLAT-uh-puss)
is just waking up.

Splash!

The platypus dives

under the water.

She twists and twirls.

She spins and swoops.

The platypus
likes to play.

The platypus is hungry.

She scoops up
a mouthful of
bugs and worms.
Yum!

The platypus has
thick, slick fur.
She has a
long, strong tail
like a beaver.

She is about as long
as a pet cat.
But she is not as heavy.

The platypus has
webbed feet and a bill
like a duck.
She lays eggs, too.

But is she a bird?

No.

The platypus

is a mammal.

People are mammals, too.

The platypus digs
a tunnel
in the mud.

Then she gathers
grass and leaves
from the riverbank.
She is making a nest.

The platypus lays
two eggs in the nest.
They are about
the size of gumballs.

She snuggles the eggs
between her tail
and belly.

Shhhh!
The platypus
is taking a nap.
She sleeps during
the day.

Uh-oh!

The platypus wakes up.

She hears a noise.

A snake is
in her tunnel!

It wants to
eat her eggs.

S-s-s-s!

The snake hisses.

Grrrr!

The platypus growls.

Are they going to fight?

No.

The platypus

scares off the snake.

It slithers away
to find food
somewhere else.
The platypus eggs
are safe for now.

The eggs hatch
in about two weeks.
The tiny platypus babies
drink their mom's milk.

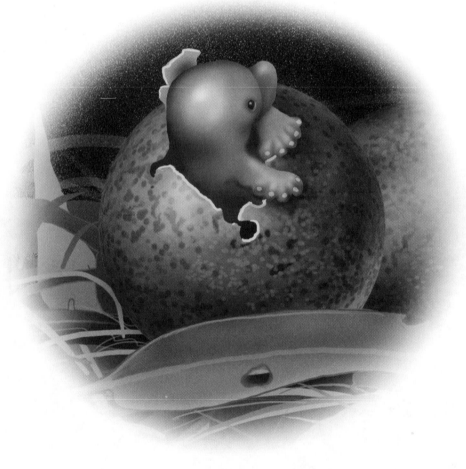

They stay in the tunnel
for four months
until they are bigger.

Now it is summer.
The babies
follow their mother
out of the tunnel.

They are hungry.
But they cannot
find food until
they learn to swim.

The platypus mom shows
her babies how to swim.
Her front feet push
through the water.
She steers with her
back feet and tail.

Then they learn
how to get food.
They use their bills
like big spoons.

Swoosh!
The platypus babies
are good swimmers now.
They zip and zoom
all night long.

The platypus family
loves to play!
How about you?